The Ta~~j~~
Fascinati~~ng~~ ~~Facts f~~or
K~~ids~~

Steven Halfpenny

This book is just one of a series of "Fascinating Facts For Kids" books. For more fascinating facts about people, history, animals, and much more please visit:

www.fascinatingfactsforkids.com

Contents

The Mogul Empire

1. From the early-16th century to the mid-19th century, most of northern India was ruled over by the Moguls, a powerful dynasty that built one of the greatest empires the world has ever seen.

2. At the height of its power, the Mogul Empire covered most of India and stretched from present-day Bangladesh in the east to Afghanistan in the west. The Moguls made the city of Agra the capital of their Empire.

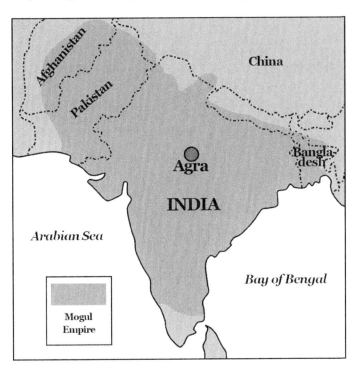

3. Although the Moguls could be violent and cruel when conquering new lands, they had a great appreciation of art, literature, and architecture. They spent vast amounts of money on great works of art and the construction of magnificent buildings.

4. The fifth ruler of the Mogul Empire was Shah Jahan. He ruled from 1628 to 1658 when the Mogul Empire was one of the wealthiest empires in the world.

Shah Jahan

5. Shah Jahan had a passion for architecture and was to spend much of his wealth on ambitious building projects. He was to be responsible for the construction of one of the most magnificent buildings the world has ever seen - the Taj Mahal.

Love & Marriage

6.   Before he became Emperor, Shah Jahan was a prince known as Khurram. When he was sixteen years of age, Prince Khurram met a beautiful fifteen-year-old girl called Arjumand Banu and they fell in love instantly.

7.   The following day, Prince Khurram asked his father, the Emperor Jahangir, for permission to marry Arjumand Banu. The Emperor agreed, but insisted that they wait five years and not to see each other during that time.

Emperor Jahangir

8.   Prince Khurram was allowed to have up to four wives, and the Emperor arranged a marriage between Prince Khurram and a Persian princess to bring the Mogul Empire and Persia closer together. Prince Khurram was also made heir to the throne, meaning that he would become Emperor when his father died.

9.   Prince Khurram and Arjumand Banu never stopped loving each other during their separation, and when the five years was up they were at last allowed to marry each other.

10.   The couple married on March 27, 1612 - Arjumand Banu was the Prince's third wife - and the feasting and celebrations went on for a month. The Emperor gave his new daughter-in-law the name of "Mumtaz Mahal," which means "Chosen One of the Palace."

Prince Khurram & Mumtaz Mahal

Tragedy

11. Emperor Jahangir died in October 1627 after a long illness, and the following February Prince Khurram became the new Emperor. He changed his name to "Shah Jahan," which means "King of the World."

12. Mumtaz Mahal was Shah Jahan's favorite wife and they spent a lot of time together. Over the years the couple had fourteen children, although seven died during childbirth.

13. In 1631, Shah Jahan had to go on a military campaign to crush a rebellion taking place 350 miles (560 km) south of Agra at the city of Burhanpur. Even though Mumtaz was expecting her fourteenth child, she traveled to Burhanpur with her husband and his Army.

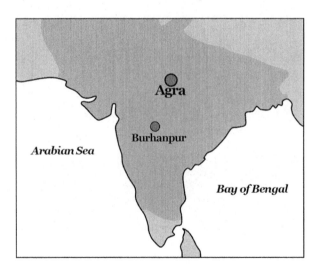

14. While Shah Jahan was winning a victory on the battlefield at Burhanpur, Mumtaz was giving birth to their new daughter. But the birth was taking too long and Mumtaz was exhausted and in great pain. The doctors were afraid that she might not survive.

15. Shah Jahan rushed to his wife's side. Mumtaz knew she was dying and made her husband promise to build a beautiful tomb where her body could lay after her death.

16. Shah Jahan promised to carry out his wife's wishes and stayed at her bedside through the night until, as the Sun rose the next day, Mumtaz Mahal died in her husband's arms.

17. As was the custom, Mumtaz's body was buried soon after she died, but it would be a temporary resting place while the tomb that Mumtaz had asked for was built.

18. Shah Jahan was overcome with grief at the death of his wife and he locked himself away for a week. When he reappeared he looked much older, as his hair and beard had turned white.

19. A time of mourning was declared which was to last for two years. Music, fine clothes, and jewelry were forbidden, and anyone who disobeyed could be put to death.

20. Six months after her death, Mumtaz Mahal's body was removed from the grave at

Burhanpur and brought home to Agra, where it was re-buried in a garden on the banks of the Yamuna River.

21. Shah Jahan visited his wife's grave regularly. It was in a beautiful and peaceful place, and Shah Jahan decided that it would be the perfect spot to build the tomb that Mumtaz Mahal had wished for.

Planning the Tomb

22. Shah Jahan chose a site on a bend of the Yamuna River to build his wife's tomb, about a mile (1.6 km) from the "Red Fort," his palace in Agra. It would be called the "Taj Mahal," a shortened version of Mumtaz Mahal's name.

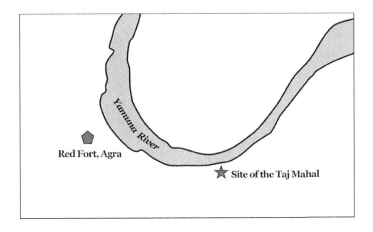

23. Shah Jahan intended his Taj Mahal to represent "Heaven on Earth," and no expense would be spared to make his vision real. By the time the Taj Mahal was finished, Shah Jahan had spent the equivalent of $1 billion!

24. The land that Shah Jahan chose to build the tomb on belonged to a wealthy nobleman who offered it to his Emperor for free. But Shah Jahan would not accept his generosity and instead he gave the nobleman a palace in return for the land.

25. Shah Jahan's love of architecture meant that he would be heavily involved in the design of the Taj Mahal, but he also employed some of the finest architects in his empire.

26. The main part of the Taj Mahal would be a huge mausoleum where the tomb of Mumtaz Mahal would be placed. Surrounding the mausoleum would be four minarets, which are tall towers from which people are called to prayer. On the top of the mausoleum there would be a magnificent dome of white marble.

The mausoleum

27. A beautiful, peaceful garden would be constructed which would contain fountains, pools, flowers, fruit trees, and exotic birds. The scent from the flowers and the singing of the birds would fill the air.

28.   Shah Jahan's astrologers studied the heavens to decide on the perfect date for work to start, and when they gave the go-ahead, thousands of workers and craftsmen from all over the Mogul Empire began work on the project. It would take them twenty years before the Taj Mahal was finished.

The Buildings

29. Work began with hundreds of workers digging the foundations for the Taj Mahal complex to stand on. Because the nearby river burst its banks every year and flooded the surrounding area, the foundations were built to enclose drainage pipes and channels which would carry any floodwater away.

30. The mausoleum, along with two other buildings, was built on a huge sandstone platform, or "plinth." Measuring 970 feet (295 m) long and 360 feet (110 m) wide, the plinth rose nearly 29 feet (9 m) from the ground to provide further protection from flooding.

31. Most of the important buildings of the Mogul Empire were built from red brick or sandstone, but the mausoleum of the Taj Mahal had to be special. It was built from white marble and stood on its own marble plinth.

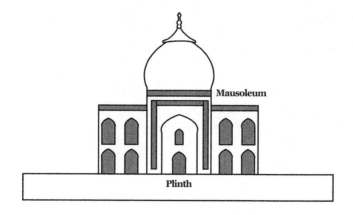

Mausoleum

Plinth

32. The marble used to build the mausoleum came from a quarry more than 200 miles (320 km) away. Teams of powerful oxen and elephants were needed to get the heavy marble all the way to the Taj Mahal.

33. Hundreds of skilled stonemasons were used to smooth down the marble and cut it into the right shape and size. They fitted the stones together so perfectly that it was difficult to tell where one piece of marble joined another.

34. On top of the mausoleum was a huge onion-shaped dome along with four smaller domes. At the center of the main dome a decorative golden rod, or "finial," was placed, pointing to the sky and soaring 240 feet (73 m) above the ground.

The domes & finial

35. Surrounding the mausoleum on the corners of the plinth were four 130-feet-tall (40 m) minarets. They were built leaning slightly away from the mausoleum so that if they fell, they wouldn't crash into the building.

A minaret

36. On either side of the mausoleum were two identical buildings - a mosque where people could go to pray, and a guest house where important people could stay. The guest house was a mirror-image of the mosque.

The mosque

37. At the opposite end of the Taj Mahal complex was a massive sandstone gatehouse. It was 75 feet (23 m) tall and looked more like a building than a gate. When visitors passed through it they would see the white, marble mausoleum shimmering in the distance.

The gatehouse

Decoration

38. The mausoleum, mosque, guest house, and gatehouse were all decorated ornately by highly-skilled artists and craftsmen from all over Asia, and as far away as Europe. Two main techniques were used for the decoration – "parchin kari" and "calligraphy."

39. Shah Jahan loved flowers and jewelry , and he got his craftsmen to decorate the buildings of the Taj Mahal with hundreds of flowers made from precious stones.

40. Using the technique of "parchin kari," highly-skilled stone cutters would carve the shape of a flower into the marble and fill the space with tiny gems which were held in place with a special glue. The gems fitted together so well that there were no visible gaps between them.

Parchin kari

41. Shah Jahan's favorite flower was the tulip - the symbol of love - and there are many of them depicted on the walls of the Taj Mahal. A single flower just one inch (2.5 cm) high could contain as many as sixty pieces of precious stones.

42. Forty-three different types of precious stones were used to decorate the Taj Mahal. They came in many different colors and from many different countries, including green jade from China, turquoise from Tibet, and deep blue lapis lazuli from Afghanistan.

43. The walls of the Taj Mahal buildings and the tomb of Mumtaz Mahal were also decorated with "calligraphy," which is a graceful and artistic way of writing.

44. Using a technique similar to parchin kari, the shapes of the letters were carved out of the white marble before the letters themselves were cut out of black marble. The black letters were then inserted into the spaces in the white marble.

Calligraphy

45. Most of the Taj Mahal's calligraphy features passages from the "Koran," the holy book of Islam. Islam was the religion followed by the rulers of the Mogul Empire.

46. The only man Shah Jahan trusted with the sacred words of the Koran was a Persian calligrapher called Ahmanat Khan, who worked tirelessly on the Taj Mahal for five years.

47. Shah Jahan was so impressed with Ahmanat Khan's work that he gave him the great honor of allowing him to put his name on the tomb of Mumtaz Mahal. His is the only name that appears in the whole of the Taj Mahal complex.

The Garden

48.   When the buildings of the Taj Mahal were nearing completion, Shah Jahan ordered work to start on a magnificent and peaceful garden. He intended it to be like a paradise on Earth.

49.   The garden would stand between the mausoleum at the northern end of the Taj Mahal complex and the gatehouse at the southern end.

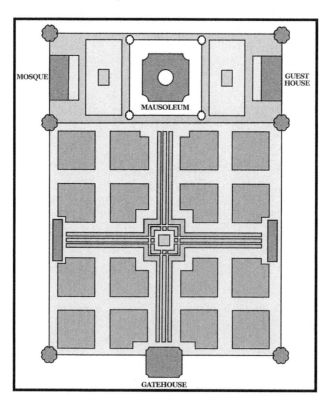

The Taj Mahal complex

50. The garden was divided into four squares separated by channels filled with water that came from the nearby river. Each of the squares was divided into four smaller squares by paths. At the center of everything was a large white marble pool filled with water.

The garden

51. The garden was planted with trees and flowers. The trees provided shade from the hot sun, and the flowers added scent and color. Exotic birds nested in the trees and ornamental fish swam in the water.

52. When visitors to the Taj Mahal came through the gatehouse into the garden, they saw the white dome of the mausoleum in the distance, not once but twice. They first see the dome itself and then its reflection in the water. It was a stunning sight that visitors today are still amazed by.

Decay & Restoration

53. Shah Jahan became ill in 1657, and his four sons fought for control of the empire. His third son, Aurangzeb, had his three brothers murdered and declared himself Emperor.

Emperor Aurangzeb

54. When Shah Jahan was well again he tried to take back his throne, but Aurangzeb had him imprisoned in his old palace, the Red Fort in Agra. From a window of the Red Fort, Shah Jahan could see the Taj Mahal, and he spent hours every day gazing at the tomb of Mumtaz Mahal.

55. Shah Jahan died in 1666, and Aurangzeb had his body taken by boat to the Taj Mahal. He was laid to rest there next to the tomb of his beloved wife.

The tombs of Mumtaz Mahal & Shah Jahan

56. The Taj Mahal suffered from decay and neglect in the 200 years following Shah Jahan's death. The Mogul Empire fell into decline and eventually came to an end in 1857.

57. Following the fall of the Mogul Empire the British became rulers of India, and Queen Victoria of England was declared "Empress of India."

Queen Victoria, "Empress of India"

58. Many of the British in India had little respect for the country's buildings and monuments. The Taj Mahal's garden was used for picnics, jewels were removed from the walls, and plans were even made to tear down the mausoleum and send its marble back to Britain where it would be sold.

59. In 1898, Queen Victoria appointed Lord George Curzon as her Governor-General of India. Curzon loved India and was furious that the British had shown such a lack of respect for the Taj Mahal and the country's other great buildings.

60. Lord Curzon began a major restoration project on the Taj Mahal, repairing the buildings and replanting the garden. When the project was finished the Taj Mahal looked much like it had done during the reign of Shah Jahan.

61. Curzon spent seven years as the Governor-General of India and when he left he said that saving the Taj Mahal was his greatest achievement.

The Taj Mahal Today

62. India gained its independence from Britain in 1947, and the Taj Mahal became a great symbol of pride for the new country. The Indian government pledged to look after all its historic monuments, including the Taj Mahal.

63. But India was not a wealthy country and many of its people were very poor. Factories needed to be built to provide employment before money could be spent on old buildings.

64. In the years following independence the Taj Mahal fell into disrepair once more, but in 1983 it was declared a World Heritage Site by the United Nations. This provided money to restore the Taj Mahal and to keep it in good condition.

65. The main problem facing the Taj Mahal today is pollution caused by the vehicles and factories in the city of Agra. The pollution mixes with moisture in the air to produce acid rain. This acid damages the stonework of the Taj Mahal and turns the white marble yellow.

66. The Indian authorities have attempted to solve the problem of pollution by closing down factories that do not use anti-pollution equipment. Only electrically powered vehicles are allowed to drive near the Taj Mahal.

Assorted Taj Mahal Facts

67. The Taj Mahal is one of the world's top tourist attractions, with around three million people visiting every year. Every month, at the time of the full moon, tourists are allowed to visit at night to see how the white marble glows in the moonlight.

68. There are actually two central domes on the mausoleum of the Taj Mahal - there is a smaller dome inside the main dome. Although the big dome looks impressive from the outside it would have been overwhelming when viewed from the inside and so a smaller, inner dome was built.

The impressive outer dome

69. In 1971, India and neighboring Pakistan were at war with each other. To protect the Taj Mahal from enemy bombers, a huge green cloth was draped over the gleaming white mausoleum to make it almost impossible to see from the air.

70. The thousands of workers who built the Taj Mahal came from all over the Empire and would have needed somewhere to live. Shah Jahan built a city to the south of the construction site where his workers could live. He called the city "Mumtazabad" after his beloved wife.

71. Mumtaz Mahal's tomb takes pride of place at the Taj Mahal, but her body actually lies in a crypt directly underneath. She is buried in a simple coffin and lies facing the Muslim holy city of Mecca.

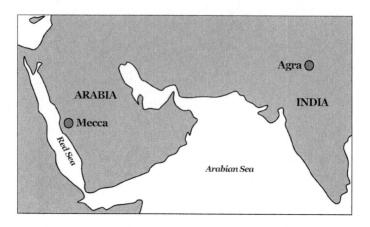

Illustration Attributions

Shah Jahan
Payag [Public domain]
{{PD-US}}

Emperor Jahangir
Abu al-Hasan (1589-1630)
{{PD-US}}

Prince Khurram & Mumtaz Mahal
Vinger World [CC BY-SA 3.0
(https://creativecommons.org/licenses/by-sa/3.0)]

Calligraphy
Christopher John SSF from Stroud, NSW,
Australia [CC BY 2.0
(https://creativecommons.org/licenses/by/2.0)]

The Taj Mahal complex
Villiers Stuart [Public domain]
{{PD-US}}

The garden
Biswarup Ganguly [CC BY 3.0
(https://creativecommons.org/licenses/by/3.0)]

Emperor Aurangzeb
Darbarscene.jpg: Cordanradderivative work:
Rani nurmai [Public domain]
{{PD-US}}

The tombs of Mumtaz Mahal and Shah Jahan
The original uploader was Donelson at English Wikipedia. [CC BY-SA 3.0 (http://creativecommons.org/licenses/by-sa/3.0/)]

Queen Victoria, "Empress of India"
Alexander Bassano [Public domain] {{PD-US}}

Printed in Great Britain
by Amazon

17843109R00031